THE EASY HOW-TO BOOK

by Seymour Reit

Pictures by
William Dugan

gb Golden Press • New York

Western Publishing Company, Inc.
Racine, Wisconsin

Table of Contents

How to tell your left hand from your right hand

First, hold this book in your hands, as shown in the picture below . . .and now watch:

The hand on <u>this</u> side is your LEFT hand

The hand on <u>this</u> side is your RIGHT hand

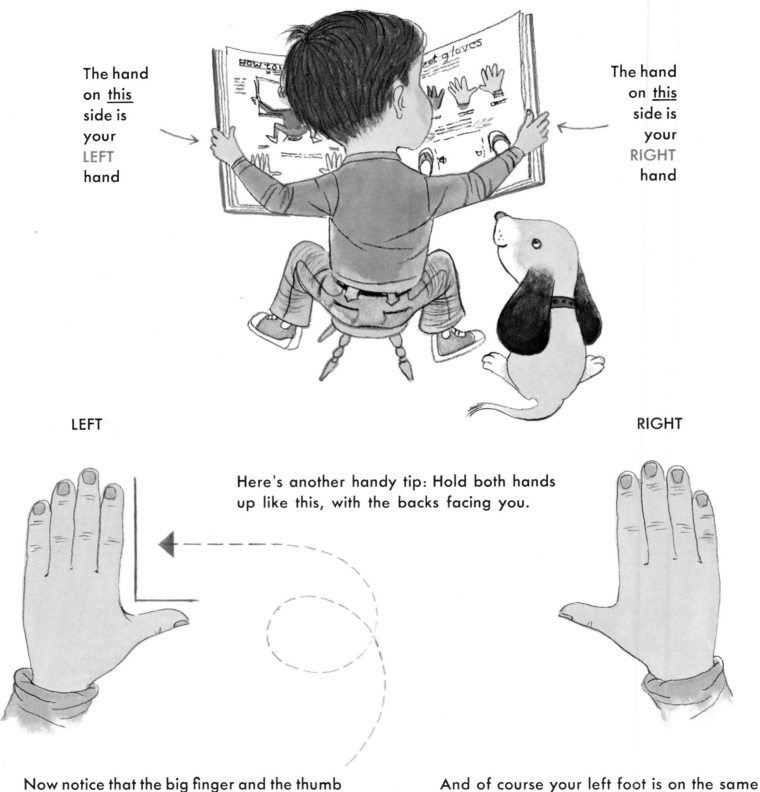

LEFT

RIGHT

Here's another handy tip: Hold both hands up like this, with the backs facing you.

Now notice that the big finger and the thumb of your LEFT hand form the letter <u>L</u> and <u>L</u> stands for <u>Left!</u>

And of course your left foot is on the same side as your left hand.

How to tell about gloves

If you put your gloves on a table with the palms down, the thumbs on the gloves will be in the middle . . . just like the thumbs of your hands

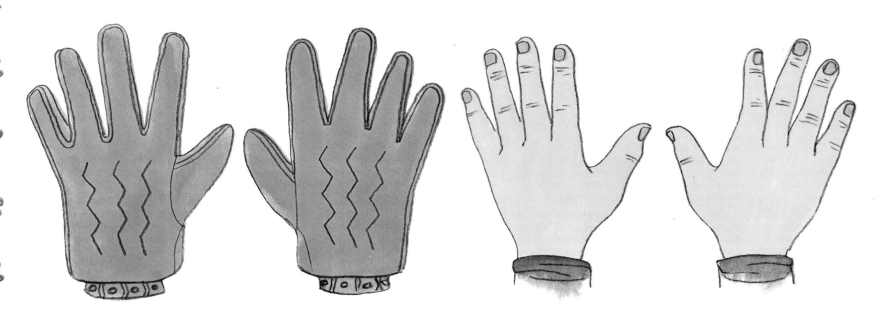

LEFT GLOVE   RIGHT GLOVE   LEFT HAND   RIGHT HAND

and it's just as easy to
TELL YOUR LEFT SHOE FROM YOUR RIGHT SHOE.
First, put them on the floor like this.

Both shoes have a straight edge on the inside.

LEFT SHOE   RIGHT SHOE

Your LEFT shoe has a curved edge on the outside.   Your RIGHT shoe has a curved edge on the outside.

How to eat an ice cream cone
so it won't drip
and get all gloppy

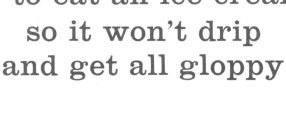

Now and then, turn your cone and lick up the drippings around the rim.

HINT: Never bite the tip end off your cone. If you do, the ice cream will melt out.

How to button a coat

If you start buttoning in the middle, you may get into trouble.

The BEST way is to start at the very BOTTOM button, and button straight UP.

how to thread a needle

(This is a tricky one!)

Be sure you have a nice bright light to work in.

Hold the thread in one hand (hold it close to tip). Hold the needle in your other hand.

Put the tip of the thread in your mouth and lick it. This will give it a sharp point.

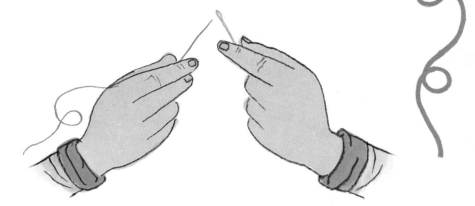

Very carefully, slide the pointy tip of the thread through the eye of the needle.

You may have to lick the thread a few times before it will work!

How to cut flowers

Never cut the flower stems straight across, like this - - ▶

Instead, cut the stems on a slant, like this - - - - - - ▶

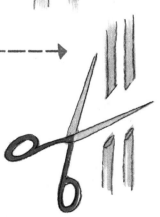

Then, when they are in the vase, they will have an easier time soaking up water.

How to care for a homesick puppy or kitten

When little puppies or kittens come to a new place to live, they may feel homesick for a few days. Here's how to help them —

IF YOU HAVE A BRAND NEW PUPPY:

Put a hot water bottle in its box or sleeping basket. This will remind your pet of the warmth of its mother's body.

Another way is to put a alarm clock in its sleeping place. The ticking sound will be very soothing.

IF YOU HAVE A BRAND NEW KITTEN:

Fix up its box or basket with something soft on the bottom (a pillow, a folded towel, or a piece of blanket). Then — if possible — keep the box near your own bed. Home-sick pets need company.

But all a homesick puppy or kitten really needs is T.L.C.

What's T.L.C.?
Tender, Loving Care!

How to tell if your dog or cat is sick

There's one very good and easy way to tell: YOUR PET MAY BE SICK IF IT DOESN'T ACT IN ITS USUAL—OR NORMAL—WAY.

IT MAY BE SICK IF . . .

it doesn't feel like EATING

or if its eyes get WATERY

or if it starts THROWING UP

or if it doesn't want you to pick it up, or touch it.

These are DANGER signs. If any of these things happen, tell your parents and they will call the animal doctor.

A doctor that takes care of sick animals is called a veterinarian . . .

. . . but most people say vet, for short.

13

How to tie a *shoelace* so it won't come untied

First, tie a regular shoelace bow.
Then take the two loops  . Hold
one in each hand and tie <u>another</u> knot in
them.

How to get a ring off that's stuck on your finger

If you just try pulling hard, it
won't help — and you might
hurt your finger.

The BEST way is to put a little
soapy water on your finger —
and let some of it leak in under
the ring.

Then—zip!—it will slide right
off.

14

How to make a peanut butter and jelly sandwich

This is easy, but there's one important thing to remember . . .

Always put the peanut butter on first. Then you can smear the jelly on top of it.

If you do it the other way around, and try putting the jelly on first—boy, will you have a mess!

How to peel a hard boiled egg

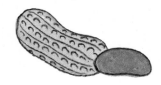

First, make sure the egg is cool. <u>Never</u>, <u>never</u> take it out of hot or boiling water with your fingers. Use a spoon.

1. Turn on the faucet and hold the egg under cold running water.

3. Next, put the egg back under the cold running water . . . and the shell will slip right off in your fingers.

2. Now crack the egg all over with a spoon, or against the side of the sink.

How to put a postage  on a letter

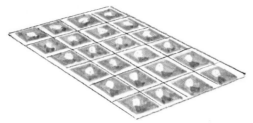

You may have postage stamps on a sheet, like this.

Or a roll like this.

Either way — first crease the sheet or the roll on the dotted lines. This makes it easier to tear the stamp out.

Next, tear your stamp out carefully, along the dotted lines.

Then lick it on the back.

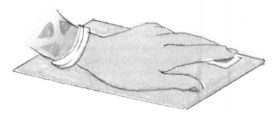

And now you can paste your stamp on the upper right-hand corner of the envelope.

How to address an envelope

SPECIAL, BIG, IMPORTANT RULE: Always print or write clearly!

Your name and address go here →

The name and address of the person you are writing to goes here (and don't forget the zip code).

Jenny Dugan
2,18 Pine St.
Phila. Pa., 19103

Miss Angela Beker
911 Pine Street
Philadelphia
Pa., 19107

The stamp goes here ←

Now your letter is ready for me!

16

How to ride a  up a hill

If it's a hill that has traffic: always ride with the cars, going in the same direction. But if you decide to walk your bicycle up, always walk on the side where the cars are coming toward you.

ride here

CAR

CAR

walk here

If it's a grassy hill or dirt path with no traffic: the BEST way is to pedal up from side to side, in a zig-zag manner. (This way, the hill won't seem so steep.)

If I did that, it would make me dizzy!

How to water plants

Different kinds of plants need different amounts of water.
Too much water can often be just as bad as not enough water.

THE BEST WAY: Ask your parents, or the florist, how <u>much</u> water to give your plant — and how <u>often</u> to water it.

Then follow directions! If you water your plant properly, it will grow and be happy.

Be sure it gets plenty of light and fresh air, too!

How to tell what poison ivy looks like

The leaves on poison ivy always grow in <u>threes</u>. There is one leaf on top, and one on either side.

In the summer, the leaves are glossy and green. In the fall, they will turn yellow, red, and orange.

Sometimes the leaves have smooth edges, and sometimes the edges are uneven.

The best thing to do about poison ivy — LEAVE IT ALONE!

If you hold both hands near the TOP of the shovel, it will be very hard work.

But if you hold one hand at the TOP, and hold the other hand farther DOWN near the shovel blade, you'll find it easier.

And never take too much on your shovel at one time!

How to lift a heavy box or package

If you bend over like this and try to lift, you will put a strain on your back.

It's a lot safer to crouch down first like this — and <u>then</u> lift.

How to pick up a puppy or a kitten

This is the best and the safest way.

Put <u>one</u> hand under the puppy's or kitten's chest (just behind its front legs).

As you begin to lift it, put your <u>other</u> hand under the back legs, to give it extra support.

This is the right way to lift rabbits, too.

How to find out how much your pet weighs

Together, you and your pet weigh ⟶ **62**

You alone weigh ⟶ = **60**

So your pet weighs ⟶ **2 pounds**

First, step on a scale and check your own weight. (Let's say you weigh 60 pounds.)

Now pick up your pet (using the way you've just learned). Step on the scale with your pet and check the weight again. (Let's say it's 62 pounds.)

The rest is easy. All you have to do is subtract the first number from the second number!

How to open a twist-off jar that's stuck

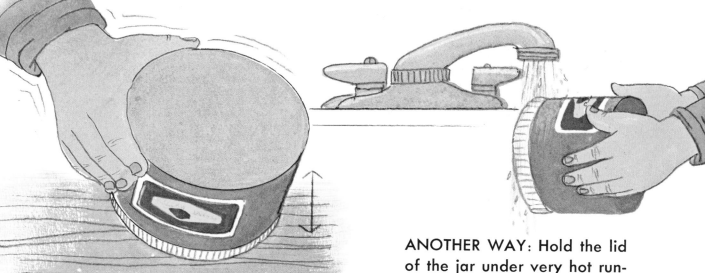

ONE WAY: Tap the lid firmly on the floor a few times. Keep turning the jar as you tap. Then try — and the lid should come loose.

ANOTHER WAY: Hold the lid of the jar under very hot running water for a few moments. This should loosen it enough so you can turn it.

These ways don't always work, but they're worth trying!

How to eat *spaghetti*

WELL, YOU CAN ALWAYS CHOP IT UP IN LITTLE PIECES. BUT THIS WAY IS MUCH MORE FUN.

Take a few long pieces of the spaghetti on your fork (but not too many).

Then *twist* the fork, winding the spaghetti around and around on it.

Now you will have a neat little roll on your fork — ready to pop in your mouth.

How to tell if it's going to rain

(Good to know, if you're going on a picnic — or to the beach)

1. The night before your outing, look up at the sky. If there is a hazy ring around the moon, like this, you may get rain the next day.

2. In the morning, look toward where the sun is coming up. If that part of the sky is very red, it may mean rain.

There's an old saying: Red sky at night — sailors'delight. Red sky in the morning — sailors take warning.

3. Take a look at the clouds. If they are soft and fluffy like this

. . . and then begin to pile up like this, rain may be on the way.

There goes the picnic!

How to slow down a sled that's going downhill too fast

Don't try turning the handle bars, because you might tip over.

The BEST way is to stick one foot over the side, and drag your toes through the snow. This will act as a brake.

How to tell the hot water from the cold water

Sometimes, the faucets are marked like this—

C for cold

H for hot

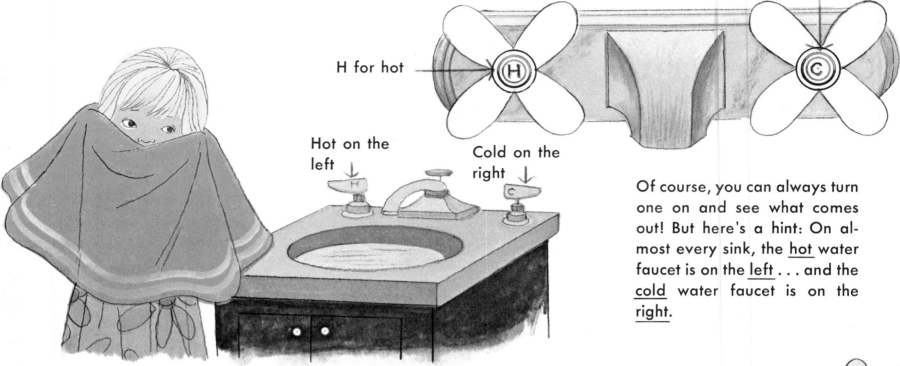

Hot on the left

Cold on the right

Of course, you can always turn one on and see what comes out! But here's a hint: On almost every sink, the <u>hot</u> water faucet is on the <u>left</u> . . . and the <u>cold</u> water faucet is on the <u>right</u>.

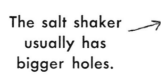

How to tell the salt from the pepper

If the shakers are made of glass, it's easy, because salt is white and pepper is grayish black.

But if the shakers are not made of glass — look at the tops.

The salt shaker usually has bigger holes.

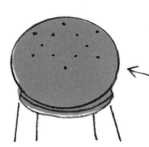

The pepper shaker usually has smaller holes.

24

How to wind a wristwatch

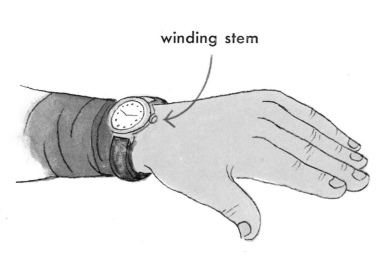

winding stem

If you try to wind your wristwatch while it is on your wrist, you may cause trouble. The little winding stem may bend or break.

The best way is first to take the watch off your wrist. Then you can easily wind the stem (using a "back and forth" motion).

How to understand about A.M. and P.M.

All the hours <u>before</u> twelve o'clock noon are called A.M.

All the hours <u>after</u> twelve o'clock noon are called P.M.

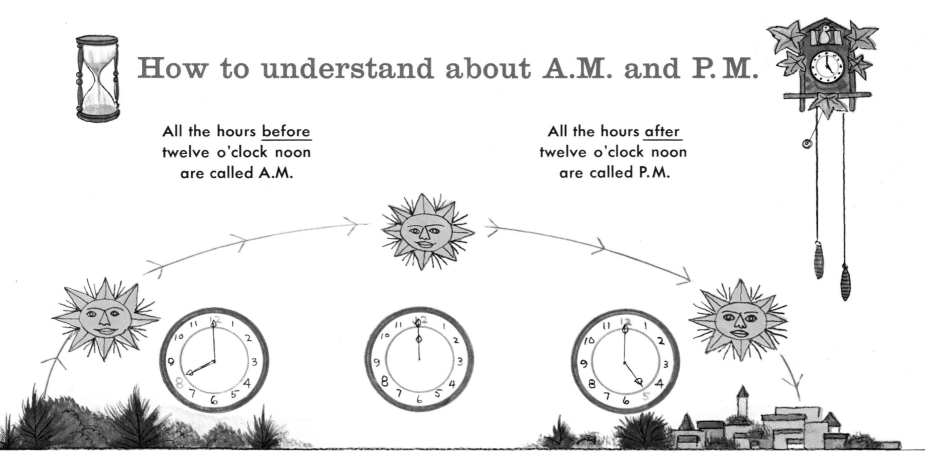

8 A.M.
means
8 o'clock
in the morning.

Noon

5 P.M.
means
5 o'clock
in the afternoon.

A handy tip: When you see <u>A.M.</u>, think of <u>A</u>ll Morning.

How to measure things when you haven't got a ruler

Question: What do you do when you want to measure something but have no ruler?

Answer: YOU USE A PIECE OF STRING.

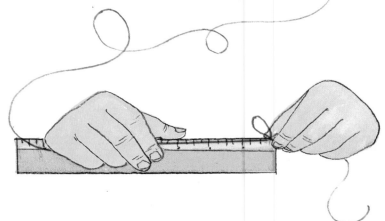

Let's say you want to find out how wide a doorway is. Hold an end of the string in one hand. Stretch the string across the doorway. Mark the spot on the string where it touches the other side. (You can make an ink mark, or tie a little knot.)

Now take the string along with you. Later, when you have a ruler, all you have to do is measure your piece of marked string. (Let's say the string measures 30 inches. So you know that the doorway is 30 inches wide.)

AND HERE'S ANOTHER IDEA—

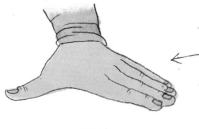

Spread your hand out as far as it will go, like this.

Take a ruler and measure the distance from the tip of your first finger to the end of your thumb. (Let's say it comes to just five inches.)

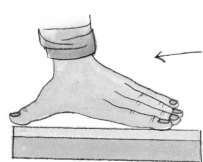

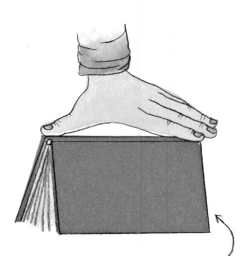

Now you have a handy "built-in" ruler, because you've learned that this distance is exactly five inches.

The book in the picture, for example, just fits your stretched fingers. So you know that the book is five inches long.

26   ("Five inches" is just an example. Remember to measure your <u>own</u> fingers — and use that length.)

How to get the ketchup out

Ketchup is very stubborn. If you tip the bottle and shake it hard, you're liable to wind up with a big messy glop.

The best way is to hold the bottle over your food with one hand. With the _other_ hand, tap it firmly on the _bottom_.

Be patient, and keep tapping firmly. Soon the ketchup will start to drip out, smoothly and evenly.

 # How to put on a Band-Aid

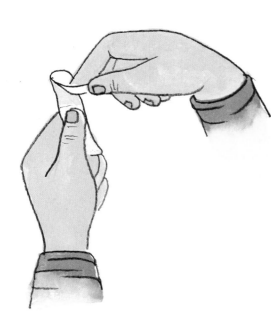

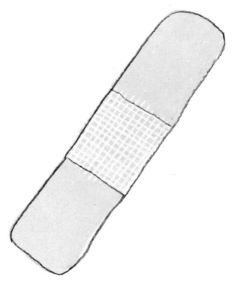

Tear off the outside wrapper first. On the Band-Aid, you will find two small pieces of paper. Peel these off.

Under the paper, there is a square of cotton gauze. On either side of the gauze, there is some sticky tape.

Put the Band-Aid on so that the gauze part covers your cut, or sore. The sticky tape will hold it in place.

27

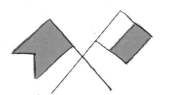

How to step into a boat

1. Never be in a hurry, and never get excited.

2. Don't step in at the edge of the boat, as this may make it tippy. Place foot in boat before putting your weight on it. Then step (NEVER jump) as far into the middle as you can. Hold on to the dock, or somebody's hand, as you step in.

3. Sit down quietly. Wait for the person in charge to tell you what to do next.

How to step out of a boat

1. Before you step out, always wait until person in charge asks you to do so.

2. As you climb out, reach for the dock, or somebody's hand, to help you. If you're carrying a bag or a package, hand it out of the boat first.

3. Again, remember to keep calm . . . never hurry . . . follow orders . . . and you'll do just fine!

How to eat a stack of pancakes

Don't leave all the butter on the top pancake. Take some of the butter and spread it between the pancake layers.

Then take plenty of syrup, or honey, or jam. Pour it over the whole stack . . . and dig right in.

How to take a good snapshot

BIG, IMPORTANT THING TO REMEMBER: **Always stand with the sun behind you.**

what you are photographing

the sun at your back

you

After you're in the right position, peek through the little finder window on your camera.

Make sure your picture is centered — and the camera is straight.

When you press the shutter button, hold the camera very steady.

HINT: Just before you press the shutter, hold your breath for a second. Then you will be less likely to jiggle the camera.

How to throw a ball

First, get a firm grip on the ball. Then as you throw it, step forward with your <u>opposite</u> foot.

If you throw with your right hand, step out with your left foot . . .
and if you throw with your left hand, step out with your right foot. It gives you better balance!

How to hit a ball with a bat

If you're having trouble connecting with the pitch,
try this little tip: Shorten up on your bat.
This often helps, because it gives you better control.

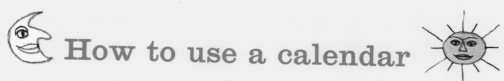

How to use a calendar

Calendars are like stories. They tell us about the days and weeks for each month of the year. A particular day on a calendar is called a date.

Days of the week

Name of the month

This is Saturday October 6th

October

SUN	MON	TUE	WED	THU	FRI	SAT
	1 *BALL GAME*	2	3	4	5	6
7	8 Columbus Day	9	10	11	12	13
14	15	16	17 *ALAN'S PARTY*	18	19	20
21	22 Veterans' Day	23	24	25	26	27 *SCHOOL PICNIC*
28	29	30	31 Halloween			

Some calendars, like this one, have special event days printed right on them.

This is Thursday, October 25th.

You can have fun keeping track of your own special events, too. Put colored circles around birthdays, school holidays, and so on.

Let's say your friend, Alan, has a birthday on October 17th. Take a colored crayon, and mark it as shown on this sample calendar.

31

How to get a swing started when you're all by yourself

If you're sitting down, push against the ground with your feet. This will get you going. Keep pushing as you begin swinging and bend your back as you pull on ropes.

ANOTHER WAY: Stand with the swing up against your back, like this. Hop up onto the seat as it starts forward. Then keep pumping with your body.

If you're standing up: First bend your knees. Then straighten them up quickly, and push forward at the same time.

Do this a few times . . . keep pumping . . . and soon you will be swinging smoothly.

But remember to hold on tight!

How to put on a sweater or a tee shirt

First, find the back. The back usually has a little label inside the neck band.

Lay the sweater out with the front down, and the back toward you.

Now gather it up in both hands, and push your head through the big opening.

Once your head is through, it's easy to slip your arms through the sleeve openings. (Do one arm at a time.)

How to soak a stamp off a letter or postcard, for your stamp collection

If you try to peel the stamp off, it will probably tear.
Here's a better way:

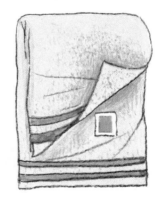

Put the envelope or postcard in a bowl or sink filled with cold water.

Let it soak there for about ten minutes. Then the stamp will slip off easily.

Put the wet stamp on a flat surface until it dries. (Drying takes about two hours.)

EXTRA HINT: Before you soak it, tear off the corner of the letter or card containing the stamp. Otherwise, ink from the address may run all over and smear it.

How to catch a baseball

Always let the baseball land in your <u>glove</u> first. Then cover it quickly with your other hand. But remember: Your padded glove will keep you from hurting your hand when the ball hits.

How to catch a football

Always catch a football with <u>both hands.</u> Then pull the ball in toward your chest. This will "cradle" the ball, and keep you from fumbling it.

Of course, if you're running to catch a pass, all you can do is reach up and grab!

How to hold a tennis racket

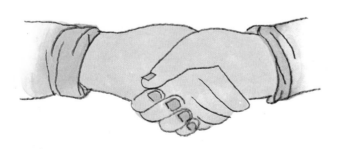

Here's a good tip: Pretend to yourself that you're shaking hands with somebody.

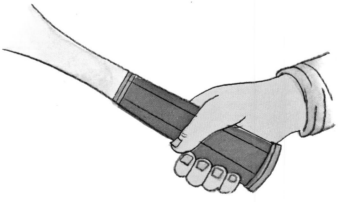

Then make believe that your tennis racket is the other person's hand! Pretend to "shake hands" with your tennis racket — and you'll be gripping it just right.

How to hammer in a nail

Hold the nail against the wall or board, just where you want it. Hold it with two fingers, near the bottom.

Tap the nail lightly with your hammer. Keep tapping until the nail is anchored a little.

Once the nail is in place, you can let go of it. Now you can hammer harder, and your fingers will be out of danger.

How to tie a square knot

A square knot is a useful and handy knot for many purposes. It is easy to tie, and it won't slip.

MAIN RULE TO REMEMBER ABOUT A SQUARE KNOT: It goes LEFT over RIGHT and RIGHT over LEFT.

Hold the ends of your rope, or cord, like this. Then put the LEFT end *over and under* the RIGHT end.

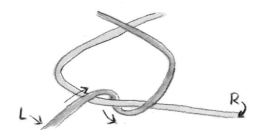

Now you simply go back the other way: Put the RIGHT end *over and under* the LEFT end!

Pull the ends tight, and you'll have a knot like this. It is called a square knot because of its square-ish shape.

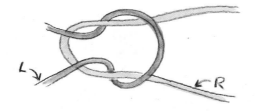

35

How to walk your dog

Whether you live in a city or in a suburb, always walk your dog along the curb.

If he's giving you a hard time, try shortening up on his leash. This will make it much easier for you to control him.

BUS STOP

How to use a big brush without dripping paint all over

Do you like to help paint fences and furniture and other things? Then remember this —

When you dip your brush in the paint can, don't dip it in all the way.

Dip to about here

Then, as you take it out, wipe your brush against the inside rim of the can.

(Don't worry. You'll still have plenty of paint on your brush, but it won't be drippy.)

How to crack a nut

Peanuts have soft shells. They are easy to break open with your fingers.

But some nuts, such as walnuts , pecans, and almonds have harder shells.

For these, you will need a nut-cracker. Be careful! If you crack the nut too much, you'll wind up with a handful of crumbs . . . Here's the right way —

2 MAIN KINDS OF NUT-CRACKERS . . . . . .  and

1. Put the nut in the nut-cracker (either kind) . . .

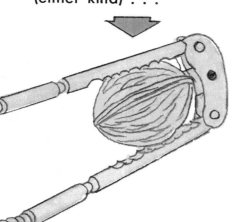

3. Crack the nut firmly, but not too much. Then take the nut out and pick off the pieces of shell with your fingers.

2. Squeeze the handles (or turn the screw) SLOWLY . . .

 # How to make a coin rubbing

Do you have a Kennedy half dollar or some interesting coins from foreign countries?
Here's how to have fun with them —

Take a clean sheet of paper and place it over your coin.

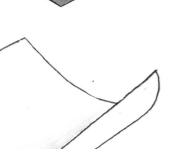

When you've finished, you'll have a magic picture that looks like this . . .

Rub over the paper *lightly* with a sharp pencil. Use the side of your point — not the tip. Keep rubbing back and forth with the side of the point.

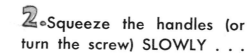

You can have fun pasting all your coin rubbings in a book.
You can also make rubbings of leaves, medals, tree bark, and so on.

How to carry sharp things

Lots of accidents happen because people
carry sharp things the wrong way.

Here's the right way —

Carry knives with the
point forward. The
sharp edge should
be down — and held
slightly away from
you.

Carry scissors closed.
The point should be
forward — and held
slightly away from
you.

Carry a closed um-
brella by the handle,
with the point down.

For campers: Carry a
hatchet or an ax just
behind the head, with
the sharp edge down.

How to butter a slice of bread
so the bread won't tear apart

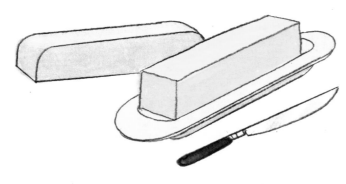

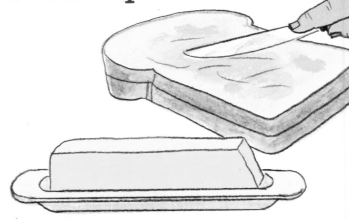

The simplest way, of course, is to take the
butter out ahead of time. This will give it a
chance to soften a bit. Then the butter will
spread easily.

Another good way is to put a second slice
of bread under the one you're going to butter. This will keep the top slice from tearing
while you butter it.

*—and never take too much butter
on your knife.*

How to pour liquids without splashing

Practice this one over the kitchen sink . . .

When you pour water, or milk, or juice, or soda into a glass — tip your glass slightly as you pour. This will keep the liquid from splashing out.

Tipping your glass is very good when you pour soda. If you tip your glass, it will keep the fizz from piling up on top.

and

How to carry liquids

Simple things to remember . . .

1. Don't fill your glass or cup to the top. If you fill it *too full*, it will splash and make a mess.

2. Carry your glass or cup with both hands. And always walk slowly.

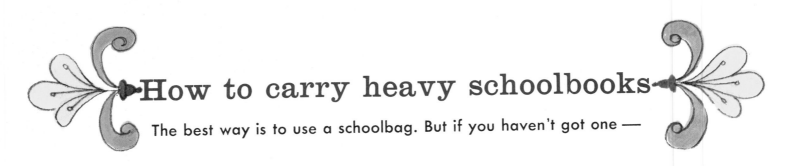

How to carry heavy schoolbooks

The best way is to use a schoolbag. But if you haven't got one —

Try putting a leather strap, or belt, around your books. Then carry them over your shoulder, like this.

Another good way is to carry them in front of you, with both arms wrapped around them. Cradle them, like this.

You can also divide your books in half. Carry half under one arm, and half under the other arm, like this.

Listen: another good way is to ask a friend to help you!

How to climb down a steep hill where there's no path

(If you try to walk straight down, you may land on your nose.)

The SAFE way is to turn your body and your feet sideways. Now bend your knees a little, and work your way down slowly. For more help, you can touch the ground with one hand. (Use the hand nearest to the hill. It will give you another "point of contact" as you move down.)

★ *EXTRA HINT: Move down at a slant, or angle, rather than straight.*

How to find your way

Wherever you walk, you're sure to find many helpful "clues" along your route. These clues will help you to find your way and to get where you're going.

- To find your way in the country, watch for —

- To find your way in the city, watch for —

barns

church steeples

road signs

special odd-shaped trees

bridges or culverts

street signs

house numbers

familiar shops

BUS STOP

416

PINE

CAN

special buildings (such as libraries and fire stations)

— AND you also have an address!

BUT—if you need HELP (and everybody does, sometimes) it's okay to ask—

A local farmer

A storekeeper

A mailman

A policeman

A cab driver

or a friendly passerby

How to carry stuff home

Let's say you've collected some pine cones, or interesting rocks, or other things, while hiking. Here's a good way to carry it all home —

Lay your sweater or jacket out on the ground, and pile your things in the middle, like this

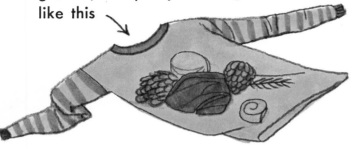

Tie the end of each sleeve to the opposite corner of your sweater, like this

Now you can lift the whole thing by the two knots — and you'll have a neat little bundle.

How to carry a friend who has fallen down and hurt his foot

Sometimes, when you're in the park or the playground, somebody falls down and hurts his leg. Or twists his ankle. If there's a third person with you, here's how to carry your injured friend home —

Make a "wrist seat." Grasp one of your own wrists, and one of the other person's wrists, to form a square. If you do it right, it will look like this.

Now your injured friend can sit on this wrist seat. He can put his arms around both your shoulders. (You'll be surprised how easily you can carry him this way.)

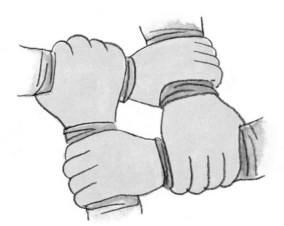

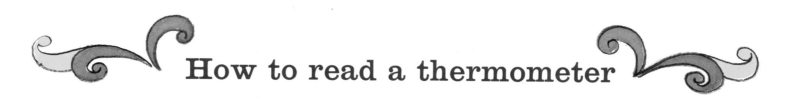

How to read a thermometer

Perhaps there is a thermometer outside a window of your house. Or attached to a nearby building. Thermometers are very useful. They tell us about the weather. They tell us how hot or cold it is outside.

The red liquid used in most thermometers is called alcohol. It has been colored red so it can be more easily seen.

These marks and numbers measure the height of the liquid in the tube.

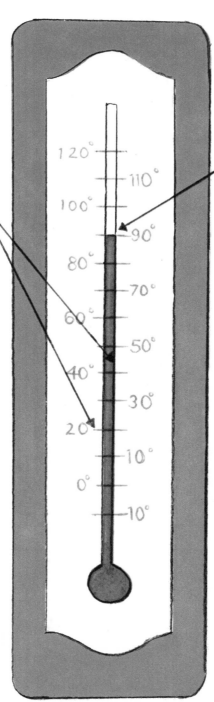

Temperature is always measured in degrees. The symbol for degree is a tiny circle next to the number.

This thermometer shows 90 degrees — which means it's a pretty hot day out.

If the liquid only came up to here (the 20 degree mark), it would be quite cold out. You'd need lots of warm clothing.

The higher the liquid in the thermometer, the hotter the weather.

How to climb down a rope

NEVER slide down a rope using only your hands. If you do, you may give your hands a painful "rope burn."

The right way is to move down the rope, holding it with BOTH your hands and your feet . . .

Keep your left foot pointing straight ahead, and turn your right foot out. Now grip the rope between your two feet. This helps you to "stand" on the rope, with one foot (left) under it and one (right) on top. See picture below.

Swing one hand down to a new spot on the rope. Then lower your other hand to that spot . . .

Now slide your feet down. Get a new "standing" grip on the rope . . .

Now move your hands down again, one at a time . . .

Now lower your feet again . . .

If you keep on doing it like this, you'll make it!

7 And before you know it, you'll be at the TOP.

6 Now your feet again . . .

5 Now your hands again . . .

4 Now slide your feet up again . . .

3 Now move your hands up a little higher, one hand at a time . . .

2 Now swing up and grip the rope with your feet. (Use the same "standing" grip, explained on the other side of this page) . . .

1 Reach out and grab the rope straight in front of you . . .

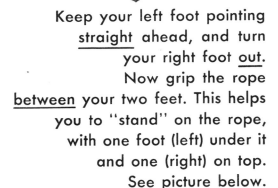

AND HOW TO CLIMB UP A ROPE read up from here

44

How to recycle things

When we recycle used items, we help to cut down waste and pollution. Here's how to get things ready for a recycling drive at your school, or in your neighborhood —

TIN CANS —

First, rinse the cans out. Then, using a can opener, remove <u>both</u> ends of each can. Flatten the can (using a hammer, or by stepping on it). Then put all the flattened cans and ends in a cardboard carton. (Be careful: Don't cut your fingers on the sharp edges.)

NEWSPAPERS and MAGAZINES—

Stack newspapers and magazines neatly in small piles, and tie a cord around each pile. You may have to turn some of the newspapers or magazines around, so your stacks will be squared-off and even.

EMPTY BOTTLES and JARS —

Rinse all bottles and jars first. Separate them by color (green, brown, or clear). Put them into cardboard soft-drink carriers. Or pack them neatly, by color, in cartons. Then tie the cartons.

When your bundles and boxes are all ready, you can carry them to the collection point. If you have too much to carry, get some one to help.

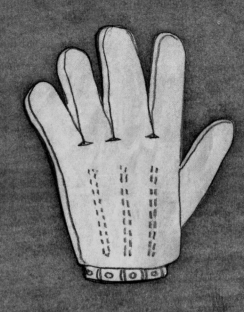
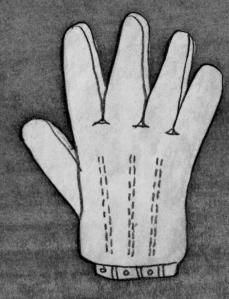

Mr. John Jones
12 Woody Lane,
Pleasant, Conn.
06605

ONE WAY